The Scientist's Guide to Physics™

Discovering
Thermodynamics

JOSEPH KANTROWITZ
AND JEFFREY B. MORAN

ROSEN
PUBLISHING®

New York

Published in 2012 by The Rosen Publishing Group, Inc.
29 East 21st Street, New York, NY 10010

Library of Congress Cataloging-in-Publication Data

Kantrowitz, Joseph.
Discovering thermodynamics / Joseph Kantrowitz, Jeffrey B. Moran.—1st ed.
    p. cm.—(The scientist's guide to physics)
Includes bibliographical references and index.
ISBN 978-1-4488-4701-3 (lib. bdg.)
1. Heat—Juvenile literature. 2. Heat—Transmission—Juvenile literature. 3. Thermodynamics—Juvenile literature. I. Moran, Jeffrey B. II. Title.
QC256.K36 2012
536'.7—dc22

                                                2010045999

Manufactured in the United States of America

CPSIA Compliance Information: Batch #S11YA: For further information, contact Rosen Publishing, New York, New York, at 1-800-237-9932.

Contents

INTRODUCTION

Boiling water is hot. Ice is cold. The contrast between hot and cold is detected naturally by sense receptors in our skin that give us the ability to sense heat and its opposite. We measure heat with a thermometer and we assign it a temperature. But what exactly is heat? What is temperature? What makes things hot or cold? How does temperature change? Why should we care if things are hot or cold? Why should we try to understand how heat moves from one place to another?

Dictionary definitions of "hot" and "cold" relate those sensations to our normal body temperature.

Warm things have temperatures above our body temperature, and cold things have temperatures below our body temperature. In this way, humans are able to compare the temperatures of things and get a subjective sense of hotness or coldness. In one sense, heat is a sensation in the mind. But we know that some physical process is causing our nerves to be stimulated in this way. What is happening in nature that causes us to feel these sensations of hot and cold?

Small, thin ice crystals form on the surface of cold objects to form frost. The water vapor in the air changes directly to a solid.

It isn't only human beings who respond to heat flow and changes in temperature. Heat affects all material objects and the environment as well. Temperature determines whether most substances exist in a solid, liquid, or gaseous state. Heating and cooling, if it changes the temperature of a

Fire was civilization's first great energy discovery, with firewood as the main fuel.

substance enough, can change the state of matter. So basic is the phenomenon of temperature that physicists consider it a fundamental property of matter, along with volume, mass, electric charge, and time.

The word "thermodynamics" consists of *thermo*, meaning heat, and *dynamics*, which refers to movement or change. In its broadest sense, thermodynamics is about heat and how heat moves and changes. The fact that heat moves at all was itself a discovery of considerable importance. It is not at all obvious. You light a campfire and it warms you. It has heat. The fire goes out, and the heat seems to disappear. Common experience will not tell you that none of that heat has really disappeared. Heat

is a form of energy, and energy can be neither created nor destroyed. That, as you will learn, is one of the most important of the laws of thermodynamics. Thermodynamics is really all about the study of thermal energy and how it behaves.

Over time, scientists and engineers learned that heat energy is related to work. The classic example is the steam engine, in which heat energy is used to boil water, creating steam to push a piston attached to a rotary shaft. The shaft can then be used to turn a train's wheels or a ship's propeller or the machines in a factory. In this process, heat energy is converted into mechanical energy. Understanding what heat and temperature are and how energy is transformed into different forms is essential to understanding the modern industrial world and how we get things done. As we shall see, much of our theoretical understanding of thermodynamics did not come about until people could examine the functioning of real machines like the steam engine.

We'll approach this subject in two parts, beginning first with the history of efforts to define and measure heat energy. Out of that effort will emerge a second, more theoretical effort to understand the nature of heat and to derive the scientific laws describing the behavior of heat energy. When you understand the laws of thermodynamics, you are powerfully armed against sloppy or fraudulent scientific thinking. You are not going to be fooled by those who claim to have invented perpetual motion machines or who claim they can run your car forever on a pint of water or who claim that nuclear fusion can occur in a glass of cold water. You will understand why these assertions can't be true, and you will understand a great deal more as well. You may even understand something about the fate of the universe.

EARLY BELIEFS ABOUT HEAT AND TEMPERATURE

Chapter 1

From the time humans discovered fire or warmed themselves in the sun, people have known that heat is important. However, ancient thinkers had no idea that heat energy was related to the movement of atoms and molecules. As we now know, all matter is made up of atoms bound into molecules, and all molecules are in continuous motion. In a liquid or a gas, those molecules move about freely. In a solid, the molecules are not so free to move around, but they still vibrate within a crystal-like structure. Add heat energy to a substance and its molecules move or vibrate more rapidly. When you touch the

People have used fire as a tool for thousands of years, long before people understood it scientifically.

substance, the nerves in your fingers respond to the rapid motion of the molecules in that object, causing a sensation of warmth. Put a thermometer into a substance, and you can measure the average motion of the molecules striking the instrument. That is temperature.

Early scientists did not understand the relationships between heat and other kinds of energy or how energy is transformed from one type to another. It took hundreds of years for scientists to develop the understanding of heat we have today.

PHYSICAL SCIENCE IN ANCIENT GREECE

We'll start our history in ancient Greece. There, a philosopher named Anaximander (610–546 BCE), a pupil of the great Thales of Miletus (624–546 BCE), considered the founder of Greek science, recognized a fact that dominated all subsequent Greek theories of nature. The world presents us with a series of contrasts and opposites. Anaximander believed that the most fundamental of these oppositions were the ones associated with moisture (wet versus dry) and temperature (hot versus cold). Mixtures of these opposites, and others, determined the qualities of various substances.

Another Greek philosopher, Empedocles (495–435 BCE), elaborated on this theory of opposites. He developed a theory of the nature of matter that

Many influential ideas in the history of Western science came from the Greek philosopher Empedocles. This woodcut illustrates his four-element theory of matter, which included water, fire, air, and earth.

described the world as composed of four basic elements: water, air, earth, and fire. Fire was believed to be the substance that made up the heavens and was considered the most rare and powerful of the elements. Since living bodies were usually warmer than inanimate objects, fire was thought to be a fundamental quality of living things—the spark of life. Although Empedocles was developing a theory of matter rather than a theory of heat, he recognized that things had different temperatures and that temperature was an important property of nature.

The Greek philosopher Aristotle (384–322 BCE) adopted Empedocles' theory of matter. Aristotle taught a wide range of scientific, philosophical, and political topics. The school he founded in Athens, the Lyceum, provided the premier education of the time. So convincing were Aristotle's logical arguments that his views on scientific matters dominated European thinking for more than a thousand years. In fact, during that long period, learning became a matter of reciting the "authorities," particularly Aristotle. Thus his teachings, including the ideas of a geocentric (Earth-centered) universe and Empedocles' four primary elements, became unquestioned facts that no scholar seriously challenged until the early seventeenth century.

Hero of Alexandria's *Pneumatics*

Though they did not understand the true nature of heat, the ancient Greeks learned to use it to operate simple mechanical devices. Little is known of the life of Hero of Alexandria, but historians believe he lived during the first century CE. By this time the Romans had conquered Egypt, and the great age of Greek philosophy was coming to an end. Hero was one of the period's last great Greek experimenters. He wrote treatises on working with simple machines like the lever, the pulley, the wedge, the wheel, the gear, and the screw. He wrote a manuscript called *Pneumatics*, which described a number of steam-powered mechanical devices. These devices included a fountain in which the pressure of steam forced columns of water upward through tubes and a device that opened and closed temple doors. In the latter device, heat from an altar fire caused air in a vessel half-filled with water to expand. This forced the water through a hose into another vessel attached to a system of pulleys and counterweights.

Hero also described a primitive steam engine called an aeolipile. It consisted of a reservoir of boiling water connected by a tube to a large, hollow sphere with open, bent tubes coming out of it.

In his book *Pneumatics*, Hero of Alexandria described a primitive steam engine called an aeolipile. The device, which existed in the first century CE, used steam power to turn a sphere.

The sphere was attached to a gimbal so that it could rotate. Heated steam entering the hollow sphere caused it to spin as it blew the steam out of the bent tubes. The aeolipile was the first device known to transform heat into rotary motion. In effect, Hero's device was the first steam turbine.

Most of the devices that Hero described served only as toys or novelties and had no practical function. The aeolipile could be used to rotate a small platform of dancing figurines, for example. The thought does not seem to have occurred to anyone in ancient Greece that such devices might be used to substitute mechanical power for human muscles. That may be because these ancient societies were based on cheap slave labor, and Greek intellectuals had no reason to figure out how to do things with less effort. All the same, these devices illustrate that people two thousand years ago recognized that heat energy could be used to do work. Neither Hero nor his contemporaries, however, describe any experiments performed on heat or steam, and they had no instruments for measuring or quantifying temperature.

GALEN'S TEMPERATURE SCALE

The Greek physician Galen (130 CE–200 CE), who established many of the accepted rules for medical practice for the next 1,500 years, made one of the first attempts to create a standard temperature scale. Galen served as a physician to gladiators, and he knew that many diseases and infections caused by injuries made people feel warmer than normal. He proposed a standard "neutral" temperature arrived at by combining equal amounts of boiling water and ice. On either side of this neutral temperature, Galen proposed four degrees of cold and four degrees of heat: The temperature of ice was the coldest temperature possible, and the temperature of boiling water was the hottest. Although he proposed eight degrees of temperature, Galen did not have a temperature-measuring device with which to distinguish those degrees. His efforts at quantifying temperature consisted primarily of putting his hand on a patient's forehead and estimating whether the patient felt warmer or colder than normal.

After Galen, no one advanced the methods of temperature measurement for almost 1,500 years. Consequently, there was little increase in the understanding of the nature of heat. Without accurate, reliable thermometers to measure and record temperatures, it was virtually impossible to conduct reliable experiments about heat and how it behaved.

HASLER'S *DE LOGISTICA MEDICA*

In the late sixteenth century, the need for an accurate scale of temperature became increasingly obvious not only to scientists but also to physicians. In 1578, Johannes Hasler published a book titled *De Logistica Medica (About Medicine)*, which dealt with the problem of finding the "natural degree of temperature of each man, as determined by his age, the time of year, the elevation of the pole [latitude], and other influences." Hasler believed that the body temperatures of people living in the tropics were higher than the body temperatures of people living in temperate regions. He devised a complicated chart that regions. He devised a complicated chart that connected Galen's eight degrees of temperature to latitude. Doctors used this chart as a guide when mixing medicines. However, they still had no practical idea about how to measure temperature.

EARLY THERMOMETRY

Around 1600, two Italian scientists, Galileo Galilei (1564–1642) and Santorio Santorio (1561–1636), became interested in quantifying the measurement of heat. To measure heat, one needs some substance or object that reacts in a consistent and measurable way to changes in temperature. This substance is known as the thermometric medium. From Hero's book *Pneumatics*, which was rediscovered and published in Europe in 1575, as well as from their own experiences, both men knew that heat caused air to expand. Air, therefore, was an obvious choice as a substance that could be used to measure temperature.

Galileo Galilei, the most famous scientist of his time, was born in Pisa, Italy. He showed an aptitude for mathematics and mechanics at an early age. After studying at the University of Pisa, he became a lecturer there, and he later became a professor of mathematics at the universities of Padua and Florence. Galileo made many contributions to the development of science, such as improvements to the design of telescopes and a body of experiments on motion and acceleration. Some of this work led him to reject the prevailing wisdom that Earth was at the center of the universe. Galileo became an early advocate of the Copernican system, which placed the sun at the center of the solar system. This landed Galileo in hot water with the Catholic Church.

Among his many accomplishments, Galileo made a device called a thermoscope, which responded to changes in temperature. In a letter written in 1638, one of Galileo's students, Benedetto Castelli, wrote:

> I recall an experiment shown to me thirty-five years ago by our master Galileo, who taking a glass flask the size of a small hen's egg with a neck around two palms in length and as thin as a barley-stalk, heated the flask with the palms of his hands and then, turning the mouth of it over into a vessel placed under it, in which there was a little water, when he left the vessel free of the heat of his hands, suddenly the water began to climb up the neck and rose to above the level of the water in the vase by more than a palm.

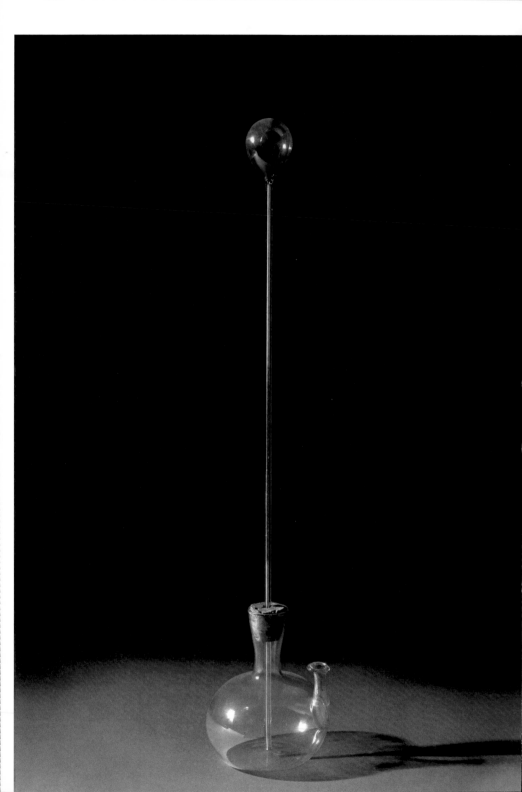

Galileo's thermoscope consisted of a relatively large, round glass bulb at the top of a long, thin glass tube. The open bottom end of the tube was placed in a vessel containing wine. When the air in the bulb cooled, the air contracted. The reduction in air volume allowed fluid to rise up into the tube. When the air in the bulb was heated, it expanded and forced the wine in the tube downward. The diameter of the tube was small compared to the volume of the air-filled glass bulb. Thus, a relatively small change in the temperature of the air in the bulb could produce a dramatic change in the level of the wine in the tube of the thermoscope. This device worked in reverse of the way thermometers work today. A colder temperature raised the level of wine in the tube, and a warmer temperature lowered the wine level.

Santorio Santorio, after serving as a physician to a Croatian nobleman, began a medical practice in Venice in 1599. He became a friend of Galileo's. In 1611, he took a position as professor of medicine at the University of Padua, where he had obtained his medical degree. Santorio performed experiments to

This is a replica of the thermoscope designed by Galileo in the 1590s. Variations in the air temperature inside the glass bulb changed the air's volume, drawing liquid up the neck to different heights.

study human metabolism. He stood on a platform suspended from the arm of an enormous balance and weighed precisely all of his solid and liquid intake and excretions. He concluded that by far the greatest part of the food he ate and drank was lost from the body via *perspiratio insensibilis*, or "insensible perspiration." Although some water loss occurs through perspiration, we recognize now that most of what we consume that is not excreted is lost as heat. But these experiments inspired many subsequent experiments on metabolism.

Santorio argued that the fundamental properties of nature were mathematical; important attributes included number, position, size, and form. His passion for describing natural phenomena numerically led him to invent several measuring instruments, including a wind gauge, a water-current meter, and a pulsilogium, a device that used a pendulum to measure pulse rate. He also produced a thermoscope at about the same time that Galileo created his. It was Santorio's idea to put the bulb of the thermoscope inside a patient's mouth to measure the patient's temperature. This was the first time that a thermometer was used in a medical setting. Santorio is also believed to be the first to add a numerical scale to a thermoscope. This was the beginning of attempts to assign real numbers to degrees of heat.

DREBBEL'S THERMOSTAT

Among the last in the Renaissance Era to experiment with air thermometers, and to try to turn them into practical devices, was Cornelius Jacobszoon Drebbel (1572–1633). Born in the Netherlands, Drebbel had little formal education and was more of an inventor and mechanic than a scientist. He moved to England in 1604 when the English king, James I, became intrigued with some of his gadgets. Drebbel devised a thermoscope in which expanding or contracting air pushed a column of mercury in a tube. This opened or closed a damper that regulated the amount of air going to a fire. If the fire burned too hot, the expanding air column would close off the fire's air supply and reduce the rate of heat generation. Drebbel had invented the first thermostat, or temperature regulator. He modified the device for various types of furnaces and ovens, and even for an egg incubator. Unfortunately, in spite of work he did for the Royal Navy on the construction of a submarine, Drebbel was regarded more as a tinkerer than a man of learning. When King James I died, Drebbel's place in the funeral procession was with the court jesters.

Galileo's and Santorio's thermoscopes are considered "air thermometers" because air was the substance affected by temperature changes. A change in the intensity of heat was translated into a volume change in the air. These instruments were very crude, however. The air inside them also responded to changes in pressure, so the thermometers also worked as barometers. This made it very difficult to obtain accurate and consistent measurements. The thermometer was not yet either a practical medical tool or a useful scientific instrument.

ADVANCES IN THERMOMETRY

Chapter
2

I n the quarter century following their invention, thermoscopes appeared in many places in Europe. However, it soon became apparent that atmospheric pressure as well as temperature affected the volume of air in these devices. Most of these early thermoscopes worked just as effectively as barometers did, but changes in atmospheric pressure made temperature readings unreliable. Those who were interested in the accurate measurement of temperature began searching for an alternative to air as a thermometric medium.

The open-ended tubes of air thermometers were frequently placed in dishes of wine rather than water. Wine did not freeze at temperatures that caused ice to form, nor did it boil at temperatures that caused water to boil. It was also known that the volume of wine increased when warmed, like air. Thus wine, or "spirits," as alcoholic substances are sometimes called, seemed to be a logical choice for an alternative to air in thermometers.

GRAND DUKE FERDINAND II'S SEALED THERMOMETER

By 1654, Ferdinand II, the Grand Duke of Tuscany (1610–1670), had developed just such a spirit thermometer. Tuscany, a region of central Italy north of Rome with Florence as its capital, was one of the places where the Italian Renaissance flourished. Ferdinand, a member of the Medici family, was a weak ruler but excelled as a scientist and a patron of other scientists.

Ferdinand II initially supported Galileo. However, he did not oppose the Catholic Church's decision to bring Galileo before the Inquisition. The thermometer

Ferdinand II, Grand Duke of Tuscany, developed the first sealed thermometer. It used alcohol, rather than air, as the thermometric medium.

he developed had the same general design as the air thermometer did—a round bulb with a long, thin tube coming out of it. But Ferdinand turned it upside down so that the bulb was at the bottom and the tube extended upward. In addition, after filling the bulb with colored alcohol, he sealed the end of the tube. With a sealed tube, the instrument would no longer be affected by changes in atmospheric pressure. Ferdinand then etched the tube with fifty equally spaced marks so that degrees of temperature could be measured. Ferdinand's thermometer scale had no zero point, however. Without a standard reference point, it was difficult to compare degrees recorded with Ferdinand's thermometers to degrees recorded with other instruments. Nonetheless, spirit thermometers began to replace air thermometers.

THERMOMETERS WITH FIXED REFERENCE POINTS

To turn a temperature-sensitive device into a real thermometer, one needs to create a scale with fixed points that correspond to common phenomena. These phenomena must be reproducible and must always occur at the same temperature. In 1661, Ferdinand's spirit thermometers reached England, where members of the Royal Society saw the importance of standardizing thermometer measurements. Robert Hooke (1635–1703), curator of the Royal Society, constructed his own spirit thermometer. Rather than begin by making regular marks on the stem as Ferdinand had, he first put the bulb of the thermometer into ice water, which he thought would be a good fixed temperature point. He made a zero mark on the thermometer next to the level of the liquid in the tube. He then made other marks on the glass tube. Each mark represented an expansion of 1/500th of the volume of the liquid in the bulb. Hooke made many other thermometers and showed that any thermometer, regardless of size or shape, could be standardized in this manner, as long as it used the same thermometric medium. Instead of wine, Hooke used alcohol with a red dye. Hooke's original thermometer was used to collect the first useful meteorological records.

After Hooke introduced the idea of fixed reference points, Isaac Newton (1642–1727) and others experimented with a long list of what they considered useful fixed points. Using a thermometer filled with linseed or olive oil, Newton put the bulb into numerous substances. The temperatures of molten metals were too high to be of much use. Putting a thermometer into the embers of a small fire produced an erratic reading. But the boiling point of water, like the freezing point of water, was a reliable measure.

Danish astronomer Ole Roemer (1644–1710), who discovered the finite speed of light, made an important contribution to the science of thermometry. When Roemer was working at the old observatory of astronomer Tycho Brahe, he found that changes in air temperature affected his astronomical instruments. As early as 1692, he used a thermometer to measure temperature so that he could compensate for its effects. Around 1702, Roemer began producing spirit thermometers of his own design. He had the insight to use two fixed points for calibrating his thermometers rather than using a single point. Roemer chose the temperature of crushed ice as one fixed point and the temperature of boiling water as the other. He divided the tube of the thermometer between these two points into sixty degrees. Using two standard reference points made thermometers more accurate. However, Roemer never published the details of his work.

THE TEMPERATURE SCALES OF FAHRENHEIT AND CELSIUS

By the beginning of the eighteenth century, scientists had recognized that temperature had profound effects on the volume and pressure of gases and liquids. Some scientists were beginning to study the behavior of gases: they believed that this line of study would reveal much about the nature of matter. At the time, the kinetic theory of matter—the theory that matter was made up of tiny particles and that the particles' behavior caused heat and pressure—was yet to be proved. To conduct the proper experiments, the accurate measurement of temperature became important.

By the early 1700s, however, at least twenty different temperature scales were in use, most of them based on a single reference point. Sometimes, a thermometer was simply attached to a board with several temperature scales on paper glued next to it so that someone reading the thermometer could use any of the several scales. Only two of these temperature scales remain common today: the temperature scales of Fahrenheit and Celsius.

Daniel Gabriel Fahrenheit (1686–1736) was a German maker of meteorological instruments who spent most of his adult life in Holland. Although Roemer never published the details of his thermometer designs, Fahrenheit heard about them. In 1708, he traveled to Copenhagen to meet the Danish astronomer and study his thermometers. After working with Roemer for several months, Fahrenheit returned to Holland and began to improve on Roemer's designs.

Fahrenheit also made barometers that used a column of mercury to measure air pressure. He knew that temperature changes caused small changes in the height of a column of mercury inside a barometer. He concluded that a thin mercury column might make a good temperature-sensitive system. Fahrenheit built a mercury thermometer in 1714. In experimental work, he showed that because the freezing and boiling points of mercury were lower and higher, respectively, than those of alcohol, temperature measurements could extend well beyond the freezing and boiling points of water. Mercury also expanded and contracted more uniformly than wine, so temperatures could be measured more accurately. Fahrenheit used the same zero reference point as Roemer had by measuring the temperature of a mixture of ice and salt water.

Because Fahrenheit was designing instruments for meteorological use, however, he felt that the boiling point of water was too high for a second reference point. Instead, he used human body temperature. He also wanted a very accurate scale with fine gradations, so he marked the tube of his mercury thermometer with 96 units, or "degrees." Later, he made adjustments to his scale so that there were exactly 180 degrees between the freezing and boiling points of water. On Fahrenheit's temperature scale, water froze at 32° and boiled at 212°. Human body temperature, one of his original reference points, was adjusted to 98.6° on the revised scale.

Fahrenheit's thermometer was the most accurate temperature-measuring device of the time. Because of its improved accuracy, the Fahrenheit temperature scale soon became widely accepted in the Netherlands and England. It is still in use in the United States. Fahrenheit used his thermometers to show that many liquids had characteristic boiling points under standard conditions and that boiling points change with changes in atmospheric pressure.

A generation later, in 1742, Anders Celsius (1701–1744), a professor of astronomy in Uppsala, Sweden, developed a new temperature scale that is still used for scientific work in most parts of the world. The idea for the scale was suggested to him by one of his academic colleagues, the botanist Carolus Linnaeus (1707–1778). Celsius divided the temperature scale between the freezing and boiling points of water into an even one hundred degrees. At first, he placed the freezing point of water at 100° and the boiling point of water at 0°, working in reverse from his predecessors. But a few years later, the scale was reversed, setting the freezing point of water at 0° and the boiling point of water at 100°. This has sometimes been called the centigrade scale.

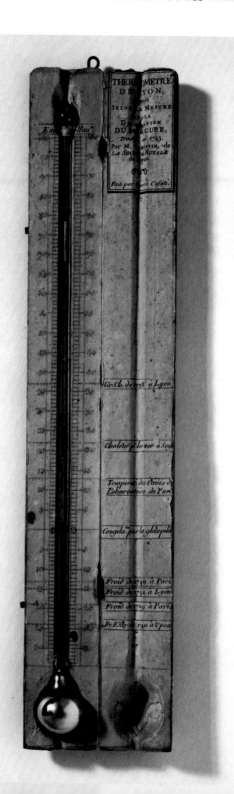

In 1948, however, the Ninth General Conference of Weights and Measures officially decreed that what had been called "degrees centigrade" should henceforth be called degrees Celsius. The Celsius scale, based on a number that was a multiple of ten, became part of the general metric system of measurements used by scientists throughout the world. It has also been used to define other scientific units. For example, the calorie, a metric unit of heat, is defined as the amount of heat required to raise the temperature of one gram or one cubic centimeter of water one degree Celsius. The Celsius degree was also used to create the Kelvin scale of temperature.

Swedish astronomer Anders Celsius invented the Celsius scale of heat measurement in 1742.

This mercury thermometer from eighteenth-century France was one of the earliest to use the Celsius temperature scale. It features a folding wooden case and a scale that ranges from -35 to 100 degrees Celsius.

THE KELVIN SCALE

In 1787, French physicist Jacques Alexandre César Charles (1746–1823) discovered that if pressure is held constant, all gases expand at the same rate as the temperature increases. He was a good candidate for this discovery because his passion was hot-air ballooning. Charles discovered that for each degree Celsius that he raised the temperature of a volume of gas, it would expand by 1/273 of its volume at 0°. Working backward, this meant that if he lowered the temperature of the gas, at 273° below zero it would have zero volume. That meant that -273° on the Celsius scale was the lowest possible temperature.

This idea was taken up more than sixty years later by the Scottish physicist William Thomson (1824–1907), also known as Baron Kelvin of Largs. In 1848, he introduced a new temperature scale that defined this lowest possible temperature as "absolute zero." On this scale, temperature is measured in kelvins in his honor.

Scottish physicist William Thomson, or Baron Kelvin, was a professor of natural philosophy at the University of Glasgow for more than fifty years. He introduced the concept of absolute zero.

CONVERTING TEMPERATURE

The Fahrenheit scale sets the freezing point of water at 32° above zero and the boiling point of water at 212°, for a difference of 180 degrees between the two reference points. The Celsius scale sets the freezing point of water at 0° and the boiling point of water at 100°, for a difference of 100 degrees between the two reference points. Therefore, 100° on the Celsius scale is equivalent to 180° on the Fahrenheit scale, or one degree Celsius is equal to 9/5 of a Fahrenheit degree. But the two scales begin at different points, so the full formula for converting between the two scales is as follows:

Degrees Celsius = (Degrees Fahrenheit - 32) x 5/9

Degrees Fahrenheit = (Degrees Celsius x 9/5) + 32

A degree on the Kelvin scale is equal to a degree on the Celsius scale, but the zero point on the Kelvin scale is set at absolute zero, where, theoretically, all molecular motion stops. Absolute zero happens to be at -273.15° on the Celsius scale. So to determine the temperature in kelvins, just add 273.15° to the Celsius reading.

Charles never published his findings on expanding gases. French chemist Joseph-Louis Gay-Lussac (1778–1850) repeated the experiments, and he did publish his work. The relationship between temperature and volume is now known as Charles and Gay-Lussac's Law in honor of the two scientists. Knowing the relationship between the volume, temperature, and pressure

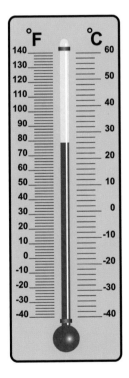 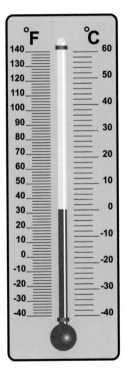 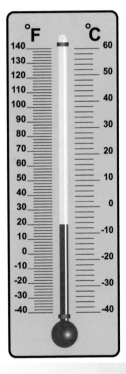

These thermometers show temperatures in both Fahrenheit and Celsius. The first one shows the temperature of a summer day in the northeastern United States. The others show low readings typical of January.

of a gas made it possible to build thermometers based on the expansion of gases.

LATER DEVELOPMENTS

In 1821, German physicist Thomas Seebeck (1770–1831) fused together two wires of different metals and measured the electrical voltage generated when the wires were heated. This "thermocouple" proved a reliable way of measuring temperature. In the 1870s, German inventor William Siemens (1823–1883), who was living in England, invented a thermometer based on measuring the changes in electrical resistance inside a bar of platinum as it was heated. By the middle of the nineteenth century, there were a number of different methods of accurately measuring temperature, most of them using the degree scales of either Fahrenheit or Celsius.

USING AND EXPLAINING HEAT

Chapter 3

By now, the relationship between heat and mechanical work was becoming a matter of interest. Engineers and inventors began to use steam power to do work and solve practical problems. One problem during the seventeenth century was the presence of water in the shafts of mines, particularly in English tin and coal mines.

The Development of the Steam Engine

Thomas Savery (1650–1715) was a military engineer who became interested in trying to solve this problem

The Engine to raise Water by Fire

Printed for T. Hinton at the Kings Arms St. Pauls Church Yard. 1747.

in the mines. He was familiar with the work of Denis Papin (1647–1712), the physicist who invented the pressure cooker in 1679. Papin observed that steam could raise the lid of a cooking vessel, and Savery concluded that steam could perform work. In 1698, Savery designed and patented a machine consisting of a closed, water-filled vessel into which pressurized steam was introduced. The steam forced the water to a higher level. When the water was expelled, a sprinkler condensed the steam, producing a vacuum capable of pulling more water into the vessel through a valve. In this way, water could be pumped out of mine shafts. Savery manufactured a number of his engines primarily for that purpose. He titled his 1702 manuscript describing the engine *The Miner's Friend*.

English engineer Thomas Newcomen (1663–1729) recognized some limitations to Savery's engine, particularly its weakness under high steam pressure. He experimented for more than ten years, finally building an improved steam engine in 1712. In Newcomen's engine, steam pressure drove a piston upward. Then cold water was sprayed into the cylinder. It condensed the steam and created a partial vacuum

The Newcomen steam engine, an improvement on Savery's engine, came into wide use for pumping water from English mines in the 1700s.

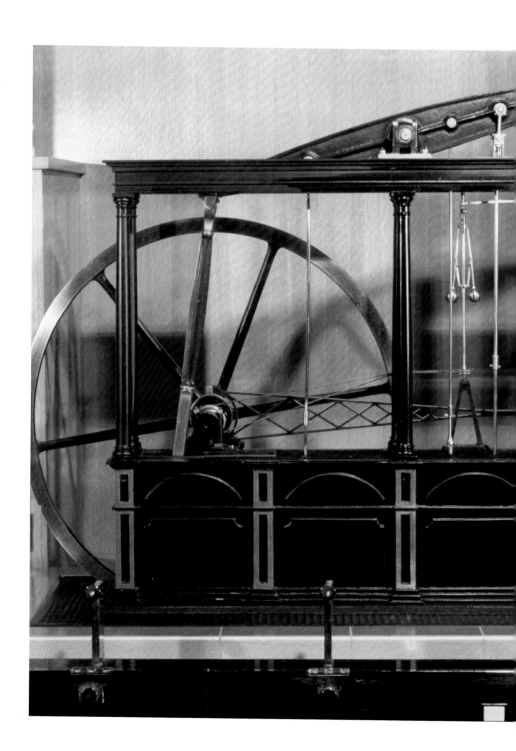

James Watt's improved steam engine, patented in 1769, drove steam out of the cylinder to be condensed in a separate vessel.

that allowed atmospheric pressure to push down the piston. Since Savery had received a broad patent for his invention, Newcomen could not patent his improved engine. But Savery recognized the value of Newcomen's improvements, and the two men began a partnership to produce better steam engines. Although the Newcomen engine was a great improvement over Savery's original steam engine, it was still only about 1 percent efficient. In other words, a lot of energy had to be used in order to pump water from a mine. Nonetheless, no other improvements in steam engine technology occurred for fifty years.

In 1764, Scottish inventor James Watt (1736–1819), sometimes given credit for the invention of the steam engine, was making scientific instruments at the University of Glasgow. A friend brought him a Newcomen engine for repair, and after returning it to working order, Watt observed how inefficient the machine was. Watt realized the problem was that the engine used the same chamber for both producing steam by boiling water and condensing the steam back to water. The same chamber had to be alternately heated and cooled. Watt saw that this resulted in a considerable waste of energy.

In 1769, Watt received a patent for an improved steam engine. The engine featured a condensing chamber that was separate from the boiler. Having a separate condensing chamber meant that the cylinder with the piston did not have to be reheated after each stroke. Oil lubrication of the cylinder also added to the efficiency of Watt's engine. Most important, Watt saw that his engine could be more than just a pump to lift water from mine shafts. He discovered how to attach a rotating shaft to the piston and convert its up-and-down motion into rotary motion. This rotary motion could turn wheels and drive belts continuously.

Improved steam engines were the main force behind the Industrial Revolution. During this period, Europe transformed from an agricultural society into an urban society, and living standards improved for many people. Steam power was able to drive machinery that could mass-produce goods. The replacement of water power with steam power meant that factories and mills could be built anywhere, not just near rivers. In 1814, British engineer George Stephenson (1781–1848) built the first practical steam locomotive, designed for hauling coal. In 1825, he demonstrated the first locomotive for a public line, which was capable of pulling multiple cars and passengers. The locomotive revolutionized modes of transportation, ushering in the modern railroad era.

LATENT AND SPECIFIC HEAT

In the eighteenth and nineteenth centuries, scientists were in a better position to study heat, its nature, and its behavior. The invention of the steam engine also inspired scientists to examine and develop theories about heat.

British chemist Joseph Black (1728–1799) was the first to distinguish between heat and temperature. He saw that the total quantity of heat within a body was not the same thing as the intensity of that heat. Temperature measured the intensity of heat, not the total quantity of heat energy. He drew this distinction in the early 1760s, when he studied changes in the state of water. Black observed that when a block of ice was heated, it melted, but its temperature did not increase until all of the ice had been transformed into water. The same thing happened when water

DR BLACK.

PROFESSOR OF CHEMISTRY, GLASGOW & EDINBURGH.

Joseph Black

turned into steam. To make these changes of state, water would absorb quantities of heat, but the heat absorbed would not be reflected in a temperature increase.

Black put equal amounts of water in two identical globular glass containers. He froze the water in one bulb and brought the water in the other bulb to a temperature just above the freezing point. Then he suspended the two bulbs by wires in a large, empty room that had a temperature of 8° Celsius. He recorded the temperature of the water in the bulbs every few minutes. In thirty minutes, the temperature of the liquid water was 5°, but the temperature of the ice remained at 0°. It took ten and one-half hours for all of the ice to melt and the liquid in that bulb to reach 5°. Black concluded that it took twenty-one times as much heat to melt the ice as it did to raise the temperature of liquid water. Black gave a name to the heat absorbed by a substance while it was changing state but not increasing in temperature: he called it "latent heat."

Black also recognized that at low temperatures, a block of iron felt colder than an equal-sized block of wood did at the same temperature. Also, at high

Joseph Black, who taught at the universities of Glasgow and Edinburgh, was one of the first scientists to distinguish between heat and temperature.

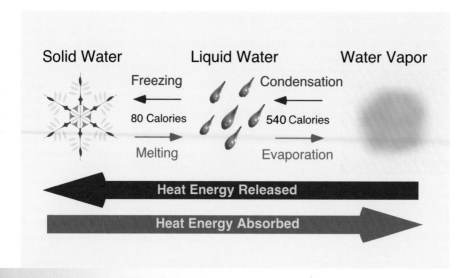

This diagram shows the amount of heat energy absorbed from—or released to—the environment when one gram of water changes its state.

temperatures, the iron felt hotter than the wood did at the same temperature. Black concluded that iron had a greater capacity than wood to conduct heat. This led him to develop the concept of "specific heat." Specific heat is the amount of heat required to raise the temperature of one gram of a substance 1° Celsius. Different substances have different specific heats. In general, metals have low specific heats. They get hot quickly. Wood and other nonmetallic materials have high specific heats and must absorb a lot of heat before their temperatures increase.

MEASURING HEAT ENERGY

We've talked about temperature scales and how temperature is measured, but how is heat energy measured? Several different units are in common usage today. One unit of heat energy is the calorie, which is defined as the amount of heat required to raise the temperature of one gram of water 1° Celsius from 14.5°C to 15.5°C. This definition shows the difference between heat and temperature and how the two are related. (Do not confuse the definition of the calorie used by physicists with the calorie used by nutritionists. That calorie is actually a kilocalorie, equal to 1,000 of the smaller calorie units used in scientific measurement.)

The official unit for heat energy in the International System of Units is the joule. One joule (J) is a unit of work or energy that is equal to the work done when a force of 1 newton (N) is exerted over a distance of 1 meter (m). Although joules are standard throughout the world for scientific measurement, calories are still often used for problems involving water. The conversion factor is 4.186 J = 1 cal.

In the English system, the unit of heat energy is the British thermal unit (Btu). One Btu is the amount of heat required to raise the temperature of one pound (0.4 kg) of water 1° Fahrenheit. To convert units, 1 Btu = 252 cal = 1,055 J.

Today, we still use the concept of specific heat. With different substances, it takes a different quantity of heat energy to bring about an equal rise in temperature. Specific heat is a ratio: it is the amount of heat needed to raise the temperature of one gram of a substance 1° Celsius compared to the amount of heat needed to raise the temperature of one gram of water 1° Celsius. The specific heat of iron, for example, is .11. It requires only about one-tenth as much heat to raise the temperature of a gram of iron 1° Celsius as it does to raise the temperature of a gram of water 1° Celsius.

The specific heat of ice is .50, half that of liquid water. This means that it should take half a calorie of heat to raise the temperature of a gram of ice 1° Celsius. This works until the ice reaches the temperature of 0° Celsius and is ready to change state into water, or to melt. It takes 80 calories of heat to change one gram of ice into one gram of water, and during that process, the water's temperature does not rise. At 0° Celsius, it goes from ice to water. There is a change of state but no increase in temperature, even though each gram of the ice has absorbed 80 calories of heat energy. This energy was what Joseph Black called latent heat.

The same thing happens when water changes state from liquid water to steam vapor. To change a gram of boiling water at 100° Celsius to a gram of steam at 100° Celsius requires 540 calories of heat energy. Even after the addition of this heat energy, the temperature of the steam is the same as the boiling water. In the case of converting ice to water, the 80 calories of latent heat is also known as the heat of fusion of water. In converting water to steam, the latent heat is known as the heat of vaporization of water.

THE KINETIC THEORY

Together, the concepts of latent heat and specific heat help make a clear distinction between temperature and quantity of heat energy. Black himself, however, had difficulty accepting the results of his experiments. He believed in a theory of heat that went all the way back to Aristotle. The caloric theory claimed that heat was a weightless, insensible fluid, called caloric, that flowed from hot substances to cold substances. However, some thinkers of the previous century, men like René Descartes, Robert Boyle, and Christiaan Huygens, had believed that heat was caused by the motion of invisible particles. Even Isaac Newton thought that heat was due to "the motion of small parts of bodies." This was known as the kinetic theory of matter, as kinetic energy was the energy of motion. But this kinetic theory depended on the existence of atoms and molecules, which, in the seventeenth and eighteenth centuries, could not be proven to exist.

In 1798, Benjamin Thompson (1753–1814), also known as Count Rumford, published scientific observations that favored the kinetic theory of matter. Thompson was an American Tory who had shown allegiance to the English king during the Revolutionary War. When the British abandoned Boston, Massachusetts, Thompson left for England. There he was accused of being a spy for France, so he left for Bavaria, where the local prince made him a count. He chose Count Rumford for his title after the name of the New Hampshire town where he had lived.

While in Bavaria, Thompson supervised workmen boring the tubes of cannons in cylinders of solid metal. The friction of the drilling produced an enormous amount of heat. The heat was continually produced while the drilling went on, in a seemingly inexhaustible supply. It did not seem sensible to Thompson that heat could exist in the form of a specific quantity of fluid. If it did, the supply would eventually run out. Heat seemed to be a product of the continual motion of the grinding process. Thompson concluded that heat must be related to motion. He performed experiments that yielded data that supported his ideas. Thompson published his findings in his classic paper *An Experimental Enquiry Concerning the Source of the Heat which is Excited by Friction*. However, his ideas did not catch on at the time.

THE WORK OF SADI CARNOT

One of the scientists who studied the operation of the steam engine was French engineer and physicist Nicolas Léonard Sadi Carnot (1796–1832). Looking at the steam engine from a theoretical rather than a mechanical perspective, Carnot observed a simplified picture of a machine with two heat reservoirs with different temperatures. The water in the steam boiler had the highest temperature in the engine, and the cool water in the condensing chamber had the lowest temperature. Carnot discovered that the maximum possible efficiency of the steam engine depended on the difference in temperature between the two reservoirs. In any machine of this type, the higher the initial temperature is and the lower the final temperature is, the greater the potential for an efficient conversion of heat energy into mechanical energy.

You can see that, if this is true, unless the low temperature reservoir is at a temperature of absolute zero, the efficiency of such an engine will always be less than 100 percent. Carnot published his findings in 1824 in his book *On the Motive Power of Fire*. He died of cholera only eight years later, at age thirty-six. For most of his life, Carnot accepted the caloric theory of heat, which said that heat was an insensible fluid, so he never fully grasped where these discoveries were leading him.

Sir Humphry Davy gives a chemistry presentation at the Surrey Institute in England. Davy's brilliant lectures became fashionable social events.

At about the same time, British chemist Sir Humphry Davy (1778–1829) performed an even simpler experiment that supported Thompson's conclusions. He placed two pieces of ice in a vacuum that had a temperature below the freezing point. Rubbing the two pieces of ice together produced friction that melted the ice despite the subfreezing temperatures. This suggested that heat could be produced by mechanical work.

Because of the widespread acceptance of

the caloric theory, both Thompson's and Davy's work remained largely unappreciated for a number of years. But in 1842, German physicist Julius Robert von Mayer (1814–1878) wrote a paper that suggested that heat and mechanical work were equivalent and that one could be transformed into the other. His actual experiment consisted of little more than vigorously shaking a container of water and showing that the water's temperature had increased.

THE LAWS OF THERMODYNAMICS

Chapter 4

In the years between Thompson's and Davy's experiments and 1850, a number of scientists were on the verge of recognizing new and important scientific laws. We call these principles the laws of thermodynamics, but what does that mean?

A scientific law is a statement about nature that has proven to be true many times over, under varying circumstances. In fact, in all of the experiments conducted, it has never been shown to be incorrect. But is a scientific law something that has been shown to be true only in the past and that might be proven wrong with the very next experiment? Yes and no. Yes, because over the course of time, some scientific laws are found to be untrue. However, this rarely happens and usually causes a great deal of debate among scientists when it does happen.

Scientific laws are broad statements about nature. But they are more than just statements that things have always occurred this way in the past. We call these statements about thermodynamics "laws" not only because they can be shown to be true in many situations, but also because if they are not true, we can't be certain about any other physical laws. Scientific laws are valid not only because they always seem to work, but also because they fit neatly into a broader network of scientific principles and offer supporting explanations for those principles.

THE FIRST LAW OF THERMODYNAMICS

English physicist James Prescott Joule (1818–1889) was a fanatic about measuring the heat produced by various phenomena, and he possessed very accurate thermometers. On his honeymoon, he measured the temperature at the top and bottom of a waterfall to

James Prescott Joule discovered the "mechanical equivalent of heat" using this device to stir water in a vessel. The rise in water temperature was related to the mechanical work expended in moving the paddles.

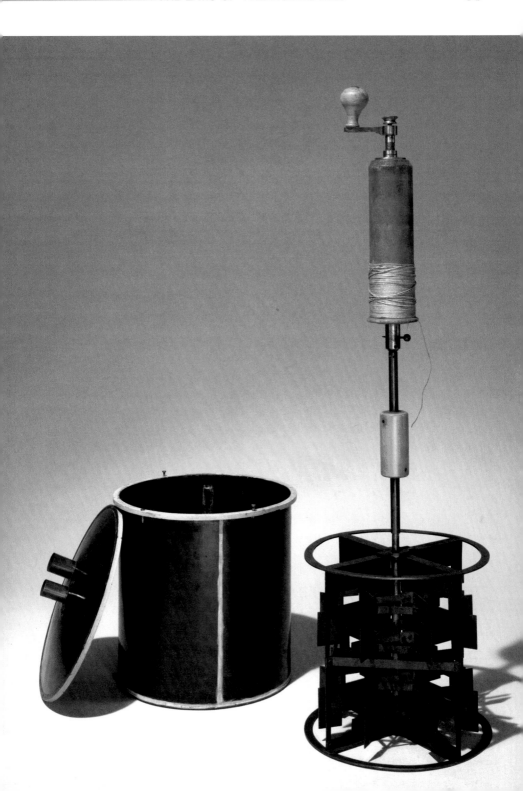

see if the conversion of the water's motion into heat energy made the water at the bottom of the water- fall warmer. Joule had inherited a brewery, and since the cellars had a fairly constant temperature, he used them to perform heat-related experiments. Joule devised an experiment in which the energy of falling weights turned paddles in water inside an insulated container. The movement of the paddles imparted the energy of the falling weights to the water, result- ing in a change in temperature.

Joule was interested in quantifying how much mechanical energy produced how much heat. By 1847, Joule had conducted enough experiments to define what is called the mechanical equivalent (or mechanical value) of heat. Joule determined that 772.5 foot-pounds of mechanical work raised the temperature of one pound of water 1° Fahrenheit. In the metric system, this means that 41,800,000 ergs of work would always produce one calorie of heat. (An erg is a very small unit of energy. It is the amount of energy or force required to accelerate one gram of mass to a speed of one centimeter per sec- ond.) Joule's calculation was not far from the number accepted by scientists today.

Experiments conducted up to this time on the motion of various machines seemed to indicate that energy disappeared as it was used. A machine might be set in motion, but if it did not receive continuous inputs of energy, it would slow down and stop. If Joule was right, however, this energy was not being lost. Mechanical energy was converted by friction into heat. Joule concluded that both heat and work were forms of energy. If heat was also a form of energy, the energy put into a machine was equal to the work done by the machine plus heat. Energy was conserved.

The principle of the conservation of energy—also known as the first law of thermodynamics—is one of the most important concepts ever discovered by science.

The most famous paper by German scientist Hermann von Helmholtz contained a mathematical statement of the principle of the conservation of energy.

The law states that the total energy content of a closed system remains constant. In other words, energy cannot be created or destroyed. Since the universe can be considered a closed system, the total quantity of energy in the universe remains constant. The earliest statements of this principle are credited to Joule and to German scientist Hermann von Helmholtz (1821–1894). In 1847, Helmholtz introduced the same idea from his studies of how animal muscle tissue produced heat when it contracted.

THE SECOND LAW OF THERMODYNAMICS

In 1824, Sadi Carnot introduced the notion that a temperature difference is required to do work. This phenomenon was studied further by a number of scientists, including French engineer Benoît Paul Émile Clapeyron (1799–1864), German physicist Rudolf Clausius (1822–1888), and Scottish physicist William Thomson, also known as Baron Kelvin. The work of these scientists led to the second law of thermodynamics, the so-called law of entropy.

This law can be stated in a number of different ways. It says that heat energy always flows spontaneously from a region of higher temperature to a region of lower temperature, and never the other way around. Rudolf Clausius stated in 1850, "When two systems are placed in thermal contact, the direction of energy transfer as heat is always from the system at the higher temperature to that at the lower temperature." Without outside assistance, heat will not pass from a region of lower temperature to a region of higher temperature.

The second law also says that in a closed system, or a system into which no new energy is added, some energy must always "run down" and become unavailable for further work. Heat energy cannot be converted back into other forms of energy with complete efficiency. Some heat energy will degrade, and the process cannot be reversed. This does not mean that the heat energy is destroyed, but that it becomes a lower-quality form of energy that cannot be used to produce work.

Entropy is defined as a state of total molecular disorder, and in a closed system entropy is always increasing. A simple way of looking at this is to think of the world as one big hill with a number of boulders on top of it. Using the force of gravity, one can do useful work by rolling the boulders down the hill. But when all of the boulders are at the bottom of the hill and can fall no farther, a state of entropy exists: no more work can be performed in this system unless some outside force supplies the energy to lift the boulders back up the hill.

The second law of thermodynamics reaches far beyond the operation of steam engines. In a closed

Some scientists believe the universe must eventually suffer a "heat death." There will be a state of equilibrium, with the same temperature everywhere. Other scientists do not believe the laws of thermodynamics apply to the universe as a whole.

system, physical processes are irreversible. The only truly closed system, the only system to which no new energy can be added, is the universe as a whole. If the law of entropy is correct, the entire universe is like a huge machine that will eventually run down. Eventually all the energy in the universe will be converted to heat and that heat will dissipate until it is evenly distributed throughout the cosmos. There will be no temperature difference between any two bodies anywhere, and no potential to perform work. This is called the "heat death" of the universe, and even today astronomers debate whether this will be the ultimate fate of the universe.

IMPOSSIBLE MACHINES

The first two laws of thermodynamics state that energy can be neither created nor destroyed, energy will always become unavailable in a closed system, and no machine operating at a temperature above absolute zero can be perfectly efficient. These laws mean that perpetual motion machines and other devices to generate limitless amounts of energy cannot be constructed.

The idea of machines that require little or no input of energy has fascinated people for hundreds of years. You may have heard about the man who claimed to have invented an automobile engine that will run forever on a gallon of water with a pinch of something added to it. Similarly, some University of Utah scientists claimed to have produced energy from nuclear fusion by running an electric current through a glass of cold water. Claims that such machines can be built should always be viewed with suspicion. Some devices make advances in reducing friction or have a design that increases energy efficiency. But so far none have been shown to violate the laws of thermodynamics. Without some external input of energy, machines will eventually slow down and stop.

Death of the Caloric Theory

As Carnot, Clausius, and Kelvin were developing the theory of heat flow, two other scientists, James Clerk Maxwell (1831–1879) in Britain and Ludwig Boltzmann (1844–1906) in Austria, resumed work with gases begun by Robert Boyle and others. They began to consolidate all of the discoveries about heat and to create a theory of matter to explain them. Previous scientists had discovered the relationship between the pressure and temperature of a gas mixture. As the temperature of the gas increased, if its volume was held constant, the pressure the gas exerted increased. Maxwell and Boltzmann, working independently, each questioned the caloric explanation for heat and explained both temperature and pressure as the effects of billions of moving molecules.

In any given sample of gas, molecules were in constant motion. Some molecules moved very quickly; some moved much more slowly. The heat content of the sample was the sum total of all these molecular motions, fast plus slow. Temperature measured the average motion of these molecules, and a temperature reading was somewhere between the fastest and the slowest molecules. Pressure also measured the average motion of molecules as billions of

molecules with different velocities collided with the measuring instrument.

The combined work of Joule, Clausius, Kelvin, Maxwell, and Boltzmann convinced most scientists that heat resulted from molecular movement. Their efforts finally laid the caloric theory of heat to rest.

Once the scientific community accepts a scientific law, scientists are extremely reluctant to reject it. The failure of scientific laws that have achieved broad acceptance has occurred only a few times in the history of science. There seems to be no serious challenge to the laws of thermodynamics on the horizon. Energy can be neither created nor destroyed. Despite the efforts of some misguided amateur scientists, you can't get something for nothing. And you cannot reverse the material processes going on in nature. Energy is used, and then it becomes unusable, and systems wind down unless more energy is added.

Individual inventors and large companies are researching the feasibility of building cars that run on hydrogen.

HEAT'S JOURNEY

Chapter

5

Once scientists understood the concepts of heat and heat flow developed during the nineteenth century, they were able to explain how heat is transferred from one body to another. The three methods of heat transfer are conduction, convection, and radiation.

CONDUCTION

People knew for thousands of years that heat could be transferred by direct contact. If you touch something hot, your hand will immediately feel hot—you may even get a painful burn. French mathematician Joseph Fourier (1768–1830) produced mathematical equations that described the rate of the flow of heat through solid objects and from one object to another. This kind of heat movement is called conduction. For conduction to take place, objects must be in physical contact. With the new kinetic theory of matter, scientists explained conduction: rapidly vibrating molecules in the hot object collide with the molecules in another object and transfer some of their momentum to these molecules, which then vibrate faster.

CONVECTION

For many years, scientists have recognized a second mechanism by which heat can be transferred—convection. This occurs when a substance such as a heated gas or liquid moves to another place, carrying its heat with it. Heated air, for example, becomes less dense and tends to flow in an upward direction, carrying heat to higher altitudes. Forced-air heating systems in buildings also work this way: a fan blows heated air molecules to another place. It is not the energy of motion that is transferred, but the heated molecules themselves. In their new location, these

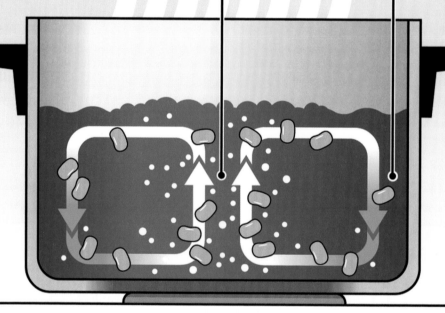

Boiling water moves the lentils around in the pot

Center of pot
Hot water is lighter than water at sides, and it rises

Sides of pot
Water cools and sinks to bottom

This movement is called *convection*

Graphic: Helen Lee McComas, Paul Trap

molecules may transfer some of their heat to surrounding substances through conduction.

Radiation

There is a third way that heat can be transferred, though the process was not clearly understood until the early twentieth century. At that time, scientists such as Max Planck (1858–1947) and Albert Einstein (1879–1955) began to explore the mysteries that James Clerk Maxwell had discovered about electromagnetism. Scientists noted that hot things were able to warm distant objects through empty space. The sun was the prime example of this, providing heat to Earth through a 93-million-mile (150-million-kilometer) vacuum. Even when you sit in front of a campfire, your body is warmed by heat energy coming directly from the fire, not through the air molecules that fill the space between you and the fire.

This kind of heat transfer is called radiation, and it differs from conduction and convection in that it

In convection, heated liquid rises to the top of a column due to its lower density. It then loses heat at the surface. The cooled, higher-density liquid then falls to be heated once again.

The hot sun constantly heats Earth through radiation. The atmosphere and clouds reflect some of the heat before it reaches the ground.

requires no material medium. No molecules have to bounce against other molecules, and no molecules have to be moved to a new location for this type of heat transfer to occur. Whenever an electrically charged particle moves, it will give off waves of electromagnetic energy.

When molecules are excited, that is, made to vibrate faster by being heated, the negatively charged electrons in the orbits of the atoms of those molecules also begin to move. Their movement is a very peculiar kind, and in fact there is no adequate physical description for what those electrons are doing. Because they "move," they give off electromagnetic waves. Some of that electromagnetic energy is in the form of light, which is what enables us to see objects. Any object at a

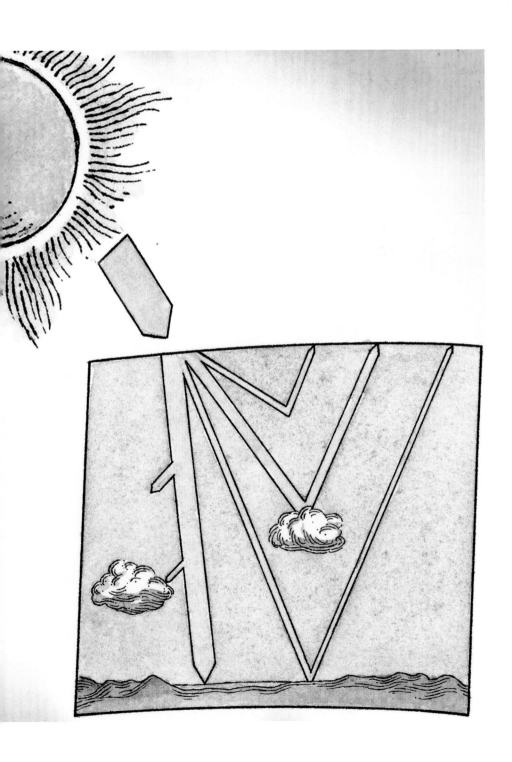

temperature above absolute zero gives off electro-magnetic radiation. An object at a temperature of absolute zero would be invisible. As more and more heat energy is added, electrons give off more energetic waves, which we perceive as a change in color of the heated object.

Some of the radiation given off by electrons is much less energetic than light waves. Just below the threshold of visible light we find a range of electromagnetic waves known as infrared waves. They cannot be seen, but they can be felt on your skin as heat.

Electromagnetic waves are a form of energy. Energy, remember, is the ability to do work, or to push or pull a mass across a distance. Infrared waves are absorbed by the molecules exposed to them. These molecules then start to vibrate more energetically, just as if other molecules had jostled them. In this way, heat energy is transported across empty space.

THE ARROW OF TIME

Scientists often refer to the second law of thermodynamics as an arrow of time, or time's arrow. In measuring the length of a board, you can start at either end. You can even start somewhere in the

ENERGY VS. POWER

Scientists work with very precise definitions of energy, work, and power. The units with which these quantities are measured reveal how they are related. Energy is the ability to do work, and work is measured as the application of a force to move a mass a distance. So units of energy are going to be equivalent to units of work. As mentioned, in the International System, the unit of energy is called a joule. A joule equals a newton-meter. A meter is approximately three feet, and a newton is a unit of mass that would weigh about a quarter-pound on the surface of Earth. So if you move a quarter-pound object about three feet (horizontally, not upward against gravity), you have performed one newton-meter of work and have used up one joule of energy doing it.

Power is a measure of how much energy or work you can do in a given unit of time. If you can expend one joule of energy every second, you are using one watt of power (named after James Watt).

middle and add the distances to each end. Each way you will get the same answer. But time is not like that. In order to measure how much time it takes for something to happen, you must start at the beginning of the event and count the time to the end of the event. If an event has already happened, you may be able to figure out from recorded evidence how much time it took for that event to happen. But you cannot start your stopwatch at the end of a 100-meter dash competition and then use readings on the watch to measure how long it took the sprinters to run that distance. You cannot start at the end of an event and measure time backward to the beginning because we go through time in only one direction, from the present to the future.

In science, an arrow of time is like a one-way street. The second law of thermodynamics states that for a closed system, or for the universe as a whole, as time passes energy is expended and becomes unavailable. It is not destroyed. It simply becomes distributed in such a way that it cannot be used to exert a force on an object and move it. This process is irreversible, unless more energy can be added to the system from

Like the progress of time in a race, the second law of thermodynamics is irreversible: Different forms of energy will inevitably be converted into heat, and some of this heat cannot be used again to do work.

somewhere else. For the universe as a whole, this is impossible.

Scientists believe that we know we are passing through time because the entropy, or disorder, of the universe is always increasing. In any physical process, some mechanical, chemical, electrical, or even nuclear energy is converted into heat. Yet we know from Carnot's studies that this process cannot work the other way. You cannot convert heat energy back into mechanical or other forms of energy with 100 percent efficiency.

THERMODYNAMICS AND THE FATE OF THE UNIVERSE

Earth is not a closed system. Our sun provides a constant input of new energy that is absorbed by Earth as heat. This heat sets in motion meteorological processes and stimulates the growth of living things. Differences in regional temperatures cause differences in atmospheric pressure. These pressure differences cause air masses to move from regions of high pressure to regions of low pressure. Thus the winds are born, and heat energy is converted into mechanical energy.

The difference in temperature between the sun and Earth can be viewed in the same terms as the difference in temperature between the boiler of a steam engine and its cooling cylinder. The heat energy of the sun is converted into useful mechanical energy here on Earth. First, plants use much of the sun's heat energy to construct their living structures. The heat energy is stored as chemical energy in the molecular bonds of plant tissue. When those plants die, they become layers of dead organic matter buried deep in the earth. Over time, this dead organic matter is subjected to intense pressure, turning it into coal and oil. People mine these materials and convert the chemical energy within them into mechanical energy for use in automobiles, power plants, and many other devices. The sun's energy is ultimately responsible for the complex order we see in living organisms and in the artifacts of civilization. As long as the sun shines, we have a renewable source of energy to maintain that complex order, and we can hold entropy, or disorder, at bay.

This does not mean, however, that we can ignore the second law of thermodynamics. As we use mechanical energy to do work, some of that energy is converted into heat and is lost to us forever. It ultimately radiates into space. If, over the long term, our rate of energy use exceeds the rate at which Earth

Solar panels in California harness energy from the sun and convert it into electricity. Sunlight is a clean, renewable source of energy: unlike supplies of coal, oil, or gas, it does not run out.

absorbs new energy, we will run out of usable energy. People will have to reevaluate the way energy resources are used to power industrial societies. Once the energy in a barrel of oil has been used, that energy is gone forever in terms of its ability to do useful work. It may take millions of years to create another barrel of oil. The sun-Earth system is, for all practical purposes, a closed system: When the Sun stops shining perhaps ten or fifteen billion years from now, no new energy transfers will sustain civilization. Life on Earth as we know it will come to an end.

The same fate may await the entire universe. Baron Kelvin first spoke of the heat death of the universe in the late nineteenth century.

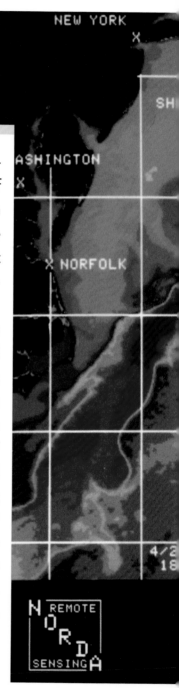

This infrared picture, taken from a satellite, shows temperature variations in the Gulf Stream, a warm current that flows through the Atlantic Ocean.

If entropy always increases, the universe will eventually reach a state of uniform temperature and maximum entropy from which it will not be possible to extract any work. What exactly does this mean if energy cannot be destroyed?

As an example, let us compare the ocean with a glass of heated water. The ocean may be colder, that is, have a lower temperature, than a glass of heated water, but the ocean contains a much greater quantity of heat energy. However, the second law of thermodynamics states that heat always flows from a region of high temperature to a region of low temperature. This means that none of that heat energy in the ocean can be made to flow back into the warmer water in the glass. With respect to the glass-ocean system, the heat

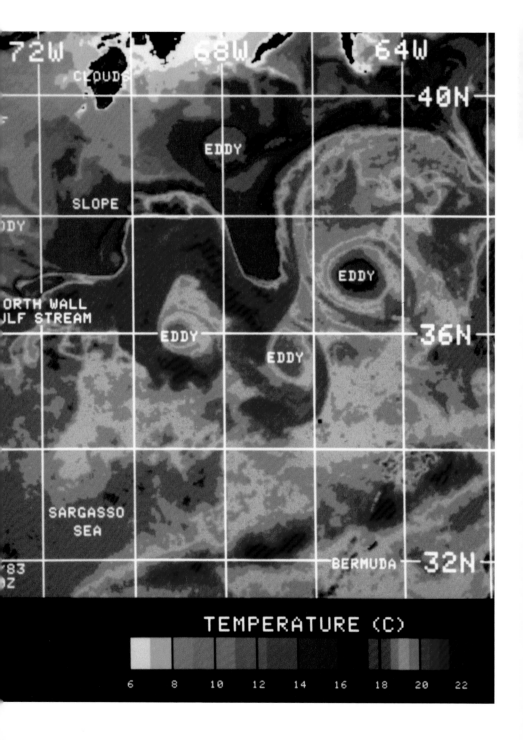

energy of the ocean cannot be used to perform any useful work. That energy has not disappeared. It has been evenly distributed throughout the ocean, and the average intensity of that energy, that is, its temperature, is too low to make heat flow into the glass of water. If the warmer water in the glass is poured into the ocean, the ocean will become marginally warmer, but eventually that heat energy will also be evenly distributed throughout the ocean. That is the state of entropy, when no temperature differential exists between any two objects, and no heat energy can be made to move in order to do work. Perhaps 100 billion years from now, that will be the state of all energy in the universe.

Baron Kelvin proposed that the laws of thermodynamics be the fundamental principles upon which all of physics is based. He believed that the laws of thermodynamics expressed basic facts about the nature of energy, force, and motion that would shape all other physical processes. Today, the idea of temperature is regarded as a fundamental property of matter, as fundamental a property as mass, length, and time. Furthermore, the laws of thermodynamics have led us to an evolutionary view of the universe. If Isaac Newton introduced the idea of a clockwork universe, Carnot, Clausius, and Kelvin demonstrated that the clock was winding down and that it could never be rewound. If the processes of energy transfer work only in one direction and are irreversible, then time, too, is irreversible. Given a closed system and enough time, all temperature differences disappear, and no heat energy can flow. Only an outside energy source can create a new imbalance, a new temperature differential, that would cause energy to move, but there is no new energy source outside of the universe as a whole because by definition the universe is everything.

450 BCE Greek philosopher Empedocles declares that all matter is made from a combination of four elements: fire, water, air, and earth.

350 BCE Aristotle adopts the idea that fire, water, air, and earth combine to form all types of matter. He claims that each element is a combination of the basic properties hot, cold, wet, and dry.

About 50–75 CE Hero of Alexandria writes *Pneumatics*, a report of his investigations of air. He describes the first known heat engine—the aeolipile—which used the jet action of steam to rotate a sphere.

170 CE Greek physician Galen proposes a standard neutral temperature by mixing equal quantities of boiling water and ice; on either side of this temperature he established four degrees of heat and four degrees of cold.

1590 Italian scholar Galileo Galilei invents a thermoscope, a thermometer-like device that measures the temperature of air in a glass bulb.

1612 Italian physician Santorio Santorio also creates a thermoscope; he is the first to apply a numerical scale to the device.

1654 Ferdinand II, the Grand Duke of Tuscany, invents the sealed glass thermometer. It uses liquid, rather than air, as the thermometric medium and is more accurate than earlier devices.

1664 English physicist Robert Hooke uses the freezing point of water as the fixed point for his thermometer's scale; he shows that a standard temperature scale can be established.

1698 English engineer Thomas Savery invents a steam engine to power a pump that removes water from mines.

1702 Danish astronomer Ole Roemer creates a scale based on two fixed points—the temperature of crushed ice and the temperature of boiling water.

1712 English engineer and inventor Thomas Newcomen makes significant improvements to the steam engine. His "atmospheric engine" converts steam pressure to air pressure using a piston and cylinder.

1714 German physicist Daniel Gabriel Fahrenheit invents the first reliable mercury thermometer. He also invents the Fahrenheit temperature scale, which is still used in the United States today.

1742 Swedish astronomer Anders Celsius introduces a temperature scale with 100 degrees between the freezing and boiling points of water. The Celsius scale is still used throughout the world.

1760s British chemist Joseph Black introduces the idea of latent heat. He discovers that when ice melts, heat can be absorbed without increasing temperature.

1769 Scottish inventor James Watt patents a more efficient steam engine, which has a second, separate chamber that can be kept cool while the other remains hot.

1787 French physicist Jacques Alexandre César Charles finds that if pressure remains constant, the same quantity of a gas takes up a greater volume as temperature increases. French chemist Joseph-Louis Gay-Lussac publishes a similar finding in 1808.

1798 American-British physicist Benjamin Thompson (Count Rumford) concludes that heat is related to motion.

1804 British engineer Richard Trevithick produces the first experimental railway locomotive.

1822 French mathematician Joseph Fourier uses mathematics to describe how heat flows through solids.

1824 French engineer Nicolas Léonard Sadi Carnot analyzes the scientific principles underlying the function of the steam engine.

1825 British engineer George Stephenson demonstrates the first public steam locomotive. It pulls multiple cars and can travel up to 16 miles (26 km) per hour.

1847 English physicist James Prescott Joule and German scientist Hermann von

Helmholtz make early statements of the first law of thermodynamics. The law states that energy cannot be created or destroyed but is converted from one form to another.

1848 Scottish physicist William Thomson, also known as Baron Kelvin, develops the idea of absolute zero, the point at which a gas has no energy. He creates a new temperature scale based on it.

1850 German physicist Rudolf Clausius makes one of the earliest statements of the second law of thermodynamics: heat always flows from a region of higher temperature to a region of lower temperature, but not the reverse.

1860s Scottish physicist James Clerk Maxwell and Austrian physicist Ludwig Boltzmann mathematically describe the kinetic theory of gases. Their equations show that the average kinetic energy of a gas is related to its temperature.

1865 Rudolf Clausius introduces the idea of entropy.

1906 German chemist Walther Nernst introduces the third law of thermodynamics: absolute zero can never be reached.

1954 The international unit of thermodynamic temperature is defined as the kelvin.

1986 Swiss physicist Karl Alex Müller and German physicist Johann Georg Bednorz discover high-temperature superconductivity.

2003 German physicist Wolfgang Ketterle cools a gas to less than one-billionth of a degree above absolute zero.

2010 A joint team of Ukrainian and American scientists proposes a new "pyroelectric" method to power tiny devices using waste heat.

Glossary

absolute zero A theoretical temperature, equivalent to -273.15°C or -459.67°F, at which all molecular activity ceases.

barometer An instrument for measuring atmospheric pressure.

boiling point The temperature at which a liquid changes to a vapor or gas.

calorie The amount of heat energy required to raise the temperature of one gram of water 1° Celsius from 14.5° to 15.5° Celsius.

conduction The transfer of heat from molecule to molecule by direct contact. Faster molecules collide with neighboring slower ones, transferring some of their kinetic energy to them.

convection The transfer of heat in a liquid or gas by the circulation of currents from one region to another.

cosmos The world or universe regarded as an ordered system.

energy The capacity to do work.

entropy A measure of the amount of energy that is not available to do work.

foot-pound A unit of work. It is the amount of work required to lift a one-pound weight one foot against the force of gravity.

force A factor that causes a body to change speed, direction, or shape.

friction A force that opposes movement between two objects or substances that are in contact.

gimbal A device that allows an object such as a sphere or gyroscope to remain level, even as its support tips.

heat The quantity of energy in a system resulting from the motion of the molecules in that system.

insensible Not capable of being perceived by the senses.

joule A unit of energy (or work or heat) equal to a force of one newton acting over a distance of one meter.

kelvin The basic international unit of thermodynamic temperature.

kinetic energy The energy possessed by an object because of its motion.

melting point The temperature at which a solid changes to a liquid.

metabolism The chemical processes by which living things grow, maintain themselves, and build new tissues.

meteorological Having to do with phenomena of Earth's atmosphere or weather.

radiation The transmission of heat in the form of electromagnetic waves, especially infrared waves.

temperature A number representing the average kinetic energy of the molecules of an object or substance.

thermodynamics The branch of physics that deals with the relationships between heat and other forms of energy.

thermometer An instrument for measuring temperature.

thermometric medium The medium in a thermometer whose property changes with temperature.

thermometry The science of the construction and use of thermometers.

thermoscope A device that indicates a change in temperature, without accurately measuring it, by showing a change in volume.

work In physics, the application of a force to move a mass through a distance.

American Physical Society (APS)
One Physics Ellipse
College Park, MD 20740-3844
(301) 209-3200
Web site: http://www.aps.org
The American Physical Society seeks to advance and distribute the knowledge of physics for the benefit of humanity. It offers information, programs, and resources for physicists, other scientists, and physics enthusiasts.

Canada Science and Technology Museum
P.O. Box 9724, Station T
Ottawa, ON K1G 5A3
Canada
(613) 991-3044
Web site: http://www.sciencetech.technomuses.ca
Visitors to this museum learn about scientific principles and physical properties while discovering how everyday technologies work. Exhibits feature transportation, communications, space, domestic technology, and computer technology. The museum also explores the role of technological change in Canada's history.

The Exploratorium
3601 Lyon Street
San Francisco, CA 94123
(415) 561-0360
Web site: http://www.exploratorium.edu
The Exploratorium teaches about scientific phenomena through explore-for-yourself exhibits, Web content, films, and workshops.

Numerous museum exhibits and Web activities explore the phenomena of heat and temperature.

Miami Science Museum

3280 South Miami Avenue
Miami, FL 33129
(305) 646-4200
Web site: http://www.miamisci.org
This museum's hands-on exhibits explore everything from
basic energy principles to the future of renewable energy.
Museumgoers can enjoy visiting the "Energy Dance Floor,"
which captures the energy of dancing and converts it to electricity, an energy garden, wind turbine, green roof, and more.

National Institute of Standards and
   Technology (NIST)

100 Bureau Drive, Stop 1070
Gaithersburg, MD 20899-1070
(301) 975-NIST [6478]
Web site: http://www.nist.gov
A federal agency within the U.S. Department of Commerce, the
NIST promotes U.S. innovation and industrial competitiveness
by advancing measurement science, standards, and technology.
NIST's labs carry out research in areas such as advanced materi-
als, electronics, and energy.

The Science Museum

Exhibition Road

South Kensington
London, SW7 2DD
United Kingdom
011 44 20 7942 4000
Web site: http://www.sciencemuseum.org.uk
The Science Museum offers rich resources for exploring the history of science. Exhibits and Web content trace developments in science and technology, covering subjects such as steam power, the history of flight, and the history of medicine. Artifacts include Stephenson's original Rocket steam locomotive.

WEB SITES

Due to the changing nature of Internet links, Rosen Publishing has developed an online list of Web sites related to the subject of this book. This site is updated regularly. Please use this link to access the list:

http://www.rosenlinks.com/phys/therm

Atkins, P. W. *Four Laws That Drive the Universe.*
New York, NY: Oxford University Press, 2007.

Atkins, P. W. *The Laws of Thermodynamics:
A Very Short Introduction* (Very Short
Introductions). New York, NY: Oxford
University Press, 2010.

Ballard, Carol. *From Steam Engines to Nuclear
Fusion: Discovering Energy* (Chain Reactions).
New York, NY: Heinemann Library, 2007.

Bloomfield, Louis. *How Things Work: The Physics of
Everyday Life.* Hoboken, NJ: Wiley, 2006.

Crump, Thomas. *A Brief History of the Age of
Steam: The Power That Drove the Industrial
Revolution.* New York, NY: Carroll & Graf
Publishers, 2007.

Gardner, Robert. *Easy Genius Science
Projects with Temperature and Heat: Great
Experiments and Ideas* (Easy Genius Science
Projects). Berkeley Heights, NJ: Enslow
Publishers, 2009.

Gow, Mary. *The Great Thinker: Aristotle and the
Foundations of Science* (Great Minds of Ancient
Science and Math). Berkeley Heights, NJ:
Enslow Publishers, 2010.

Gregersen, Erik. *The Britannica Guide to Heat,
Force, and Motion* (Physics Explained). New
York, NY: Britannica Educational Publishing

in association with Rosen Educational Services, 2011.

Griffith, W. Thomas, and Juliet Wain Brosing. *The Physics of Everyday Phenomena: A Conceptual Introduction to Physics*. New York, NY: McGraw-Hill, 2012.

Langone, John, Bruce Stutz, and Andrea Gianopoulos. *Theories for Everything: An Illustrated History of Science from the Invention of Numbers to String Theory*. Washington, DC: National Geographic, 2006.

Magloff, Lisa. *Experiments with Heat and Energy (Cool Science)*. New York, NY: Gareth Stevens Publishing, 2010.

McCarthy, Rose. *The Laws of Thermodynamics: Understanding Heat and Energy Transfers (Library of Physics)*. New York, NY: Rosen Publishing Group, 2005.

Myers, Richard L. *The Basics of Physics* (Basics of the Hard Sciences). Westport, CT: Greenwood Press, 2006.

Parker, Barry. *Science 101: Physics*. New York, NY: Collins, 2007.

Parker, Steve. *Heat and Energy*. Philadelphia, PA: Chelsea House, 2005.

Pickover, Clifford A. *Archimedes to Hawking: Laws of Science and the Great Minds Behind*

Them. New York, NY: Oxford University Press, 2008.

Rosen, William. *The Most Powerful Idea in the World: A Story of Steam, Industry, and Invention.* New York, NY: Random House, 2010.

Viegas, Jennifer. *The Laws of Thermodynamics: An Anthology of Current Thought* (Contemporary Discourse in the Field of Physics). New York, NY: Rosen Publishing Group, 2006.

Whiting, Jim. *James Watt and the Steam Engine* (Uncharted, Unexplored, and Unexplained). Hockessin, DE: Mitchell Lane Publishers, 2006.

ABOUT THE AUTHORS

Joseph Kantrowitz is a writer and science educator in Pennsylvania.

Jeffrey B. Moran has a Ph.D. from the University of Arkansas and has taught and conducted research in physiology, anatomy, and biochemistry. He has developed K–12 curriculum materials in all areas of science and is the composer of numerous songs about a wide range of scientific topics.

PHOTO CREDITS

Cover, back cover, interior graphics, pp. 4. 5, 6–7, 41 Shutterstock; p. 11 Roy H. Anderson/National Geographic Image Collection/Getty Images; pp. 13, 65 The Granger Collection; pp. 16–17 © Mary Evans Picture Library/Edwin Wallace/The Image Works; p. 22 Museo Galileo, Institute and Museum of the History of Science, Florence: Photo Franca Principe; p. 29 Galleria Palatina, Palazzo Pitti, Florence, Italy/The Bridgeman Art Library; p. 36 SSPL via Getty Images; p. 37 New York Public Library Picture Collection/Photo Researchers; p. 38 Private Collection/ The Stapleton Collection/The Bridgeman Art Library; p. 44 HIP/ Art Resource; pp. 46–47 Jean-Loup Chamet/Photo Researchers; p. 50 Michael Pidwirny, www.our-planet-earth.net; pp. 52, 63, 88–89 Science & Society Picture Library/SSPL/Getty Images; pp. 58–59 Science Source/Photo Researchers; pp. 68–69 NASA; p. 72 Jay Directo/AFP/Getty Images; p. 76 Trap/Newscom; pp. 78–79 Eugene Fleurey © Dorling Kindersley; p. 83 Black 100/ Allsport Concepts/Getty Images; pp. 86–87 Thinkstock.

Editor: Andrea Sclarow; Photo Researcher: Marty Levick